STRONG AS A LION, LIGHT AS AN EAGLE

BY MARCIA FISHMAN
Illustrated by Roberta Collier-Morales

Strong as a Lion, Light as an Eagle

Written by Marcia Fishman
Illustrated by Roberta Collier-Morales

Published by
Operation Outreach-USA Press
Holliston, MA

ISBN 978-0-9906882-1-1

Printed in the United States of America

MIX
Paper from
responsible sources
FSC® C103525

FSC
www.fsc.org

DEDICATION

I dedicate this book to Chanoch Hadar, who continually inspires me to be as strong as a lion, as light as an eagle, as bold as a leopard and as swift as a deer. M.F.

PREFACE

Growing up in Johannesburg, we ventured on safari in the huge Kruger National Park. As the untouched, majestic wilderness unrolled before my young eyes, I would dream of jumping out of our car and diving into the bush to live the "wild life".

I settled for studying the Kruger literature on the animals, but the more I drank in the information, the thirstier I got.

I still feel that I belong to that community where differences thread a woven, rustic master-piece of endless beauty. I had the pleasure of introducing Marcia to the community, and she, too, instantly became its ardent citizen.

Chanoch Hadar

On a warm, dry day in a small kraal in the bush of South Africa, a brother

and sister, Makalo and Nandi, appeared from their one-room house with a thatched roof, clay walls and dirt

floor. Their father and village Chief, Vusi, was painting a picture on a flat slab of rock. Vusi carefully dipped

his porcupine quill brush in an upturned tortoise shell which held paint made from sun-colored stones,

crushed to a powder and mixed with animal fat. The children looked over his shoulder and asked why he

chose to paint a lion, an eagle, a leopard and a deer.

1

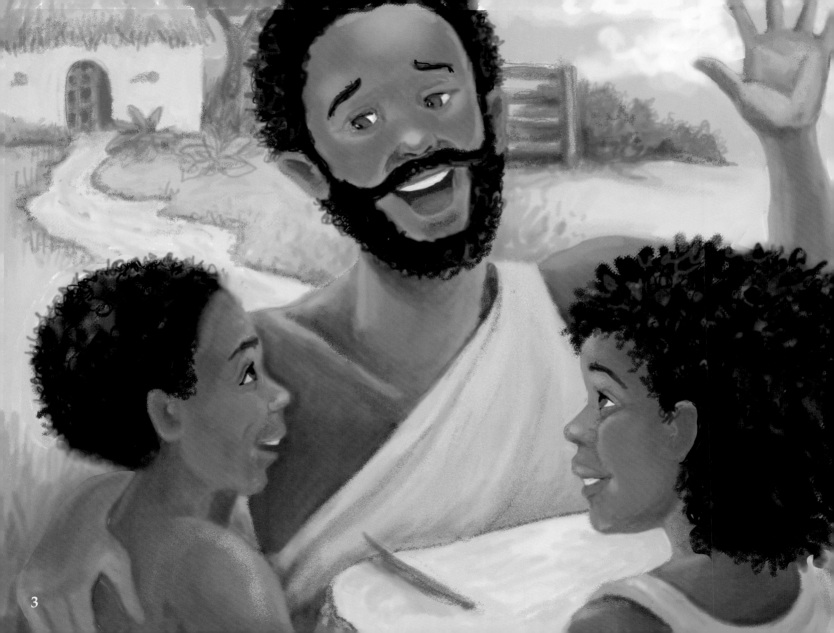

Vusi replied that he was thinking about an old story taught by very wise men.

These men said that people should live each day as strong as a lion, as light as an

eagle, as swift as a deer, and as bold as a leopard.

"No one can be all of that!" cried the children.

"Ah…but they can. Listen…" answered Vusi.

In Zulu, his tribal language, he began: Kwesukasukela….

4

…There lived a lion, named Chief Umfundi, who ruled over the African bush. Umfundi

had twin cubs named Mandla and Taki.

5

One morning, the sun peeked over Kruger Park and it was time for the twins to rise.

As always, Taki jumped out of bed at the sight of first light. Mandla loved to linger, snug

like a bug under his covers.

6

Their father beckoned them to breakfast, and even Mandla knew not to dawdle when their father called to them. While eating their breakfast of springbok biltong, Chief Umfundi proclaimed, "It is time for me to decide which of you will take my place and be the next Chief. I must choose while you are young so that I can prepare you as you grow up. I will have my decision by the end of today."

8

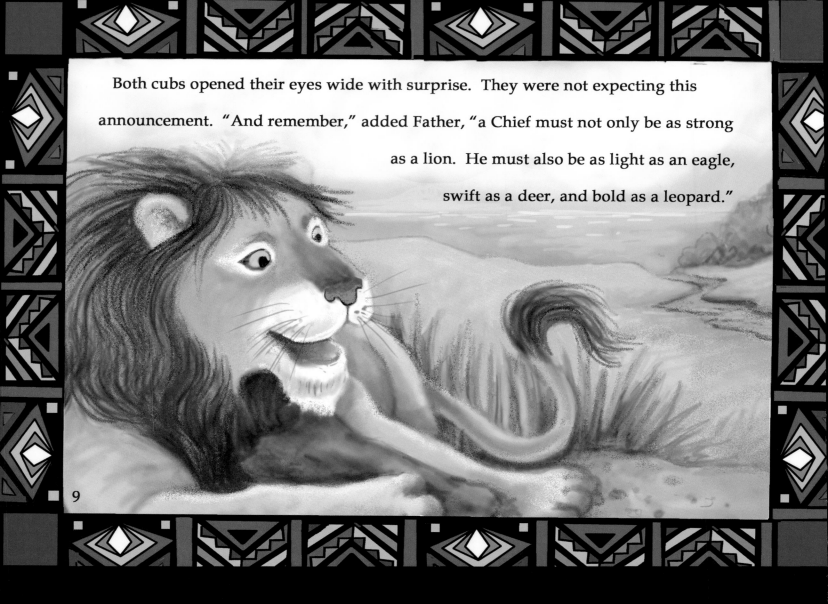

Both cubs opened their eyes wide with surprise. They were not expecting this announcement. "And remember," added Father, "a Chief must not only be as strong as a lion. He must also be as light as an eagle, swift as a deer, and bold as a leopard."

9

The twin cubs set out for their daily activities, already certain who would be chosen as the next Chief. Both knew that Mandla was bigger, stronger and faster than Taki. In fact, Taki often depended on Mandla's help when he found himself in trouble in the bush, and he even bragged about Mandla's athletic abilities.

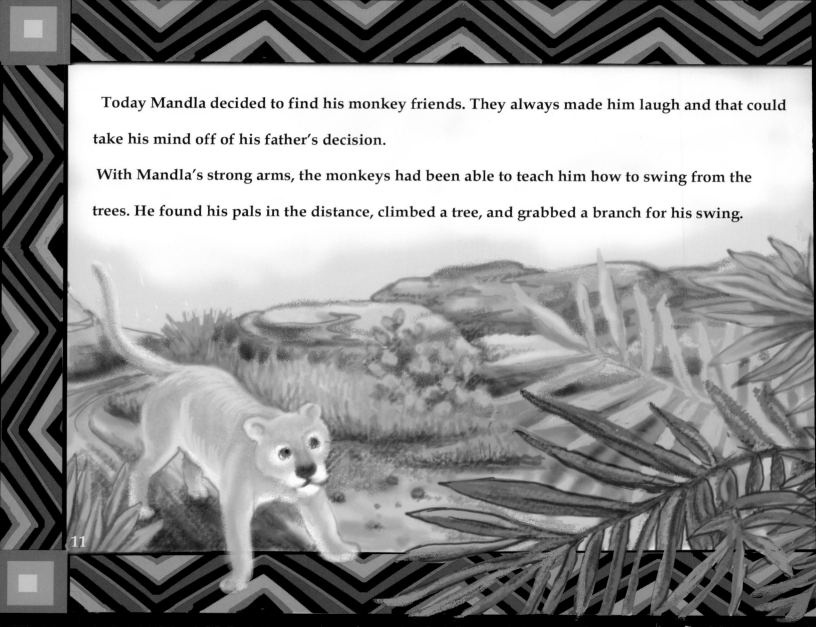

Today Mandla decided to find his monkey friends. They always made him laugh and that could take his mind off of his father's decision.

With Mandla's strong arms, the monkeys had been able to teach him how to swing from the trees. He found his pals in the distance, climbed a tree, and grabbed a branch for his swing.

12

As he swooped from tree to tree, Mandla squealed in delight, "Wheeeee…I am flying. I am surely as light as an eagle." He soared until he reached the monkeys. The monkeys were jumping up and down, arms flailing, mouths screeching and chattering away. "Whoop, whoop, whoop! Eee…oo…ha..ha..ha!"

One monkey cried out, "Mandla, watch this." The monkeys were tossing coconuts every which way. One coconut smashed on a nearby tree, another was thrown in the air and, when it hit a branch above, coconut milk spilled over the monkeys' heads.

A small hedgehog was sitting down below. When he was spotted, one monkey threw the coconut on a rock, hoping the milk would spray the hedgehog. As planned, the coconut did split and the milk did splatter, and the unhappy hedgehog curled in a ball, wet and sticky.

15

Mandla told the monkey that it wasn't nice to throw coconuts at others. "I didn't throw the coconut on the hedgehog," smirked the monkey. "I threw the coconut against the rock and the milk just happened to spray him." Although Mandla really didn't approve of this monkey business, he continued to play with them because he always had lots of fun.

While Mandla played with the monkeys, Taki sought out his very special friend, Nomsa the elephant. Nomsa was so big and strong that she could push trees to the ground and then drink from the roots of those trees. Each time Nomsa spotted Taki, she would invite him for a ride on her back.

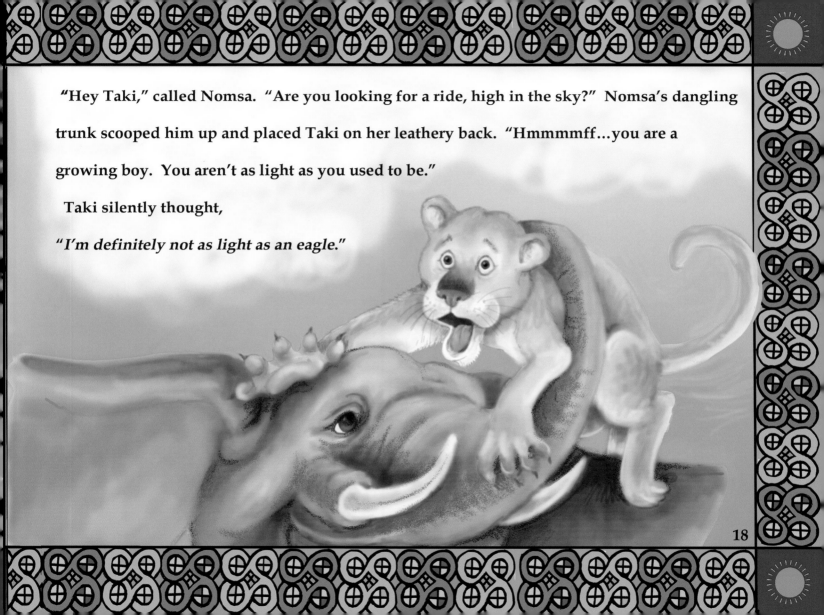

"Hey Taki," called Nomsa. "Are you looking for a ride, high in the sky?" Nomsa's dangling

trunk scooped him up and placed Taki on her leathery back. "Hmmmmff…you are a

growing boy. You aren't as light as you used to be."

Taki silently thought,

"I'm definitely not as light as an eagle."

18

19

Nomsa approached a tree and pushed and pushed. Taki pretended to help by sitting near her head and shoving with his paws. But Taki knew that he may never have the real strength of a lion. While atop Nomsa's back, Taki waved to some of his lion cub friends who were trotting down the road. "Hey, Taki," shouted one of them. "We are headed for the lake near the wild date palm tree. Come join us."

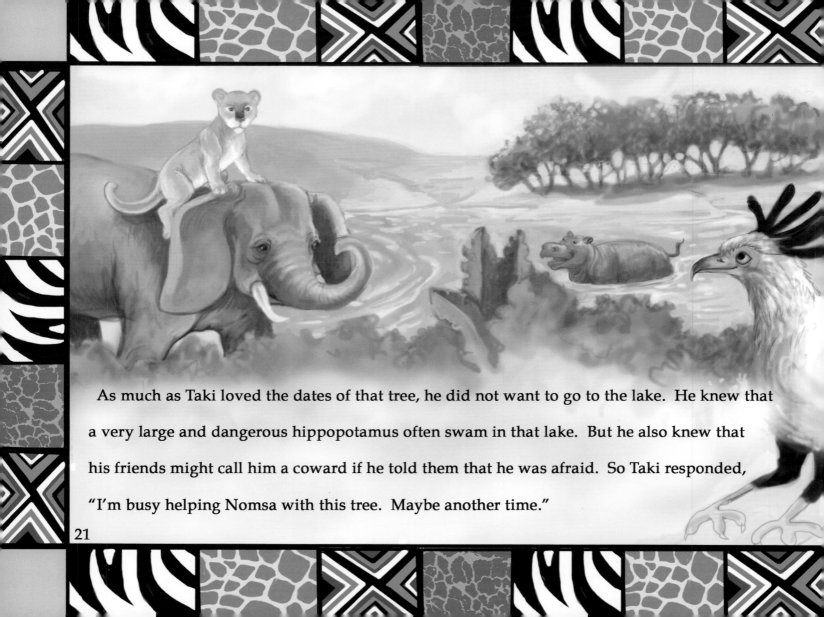

As much as Taki loved the dates of that tree, he did not want to go to the lake. He knew that a very large and dangerous hippopotamus often swam in that lake. But he also knew that his friends might call him a coward if he told them that he was afraid. So Taki responded, "I'm busy helping Nomsa with this tree. Maybe another time."

The sun began to disappear beneath the horizon, and the twins knew that it was time to return home.

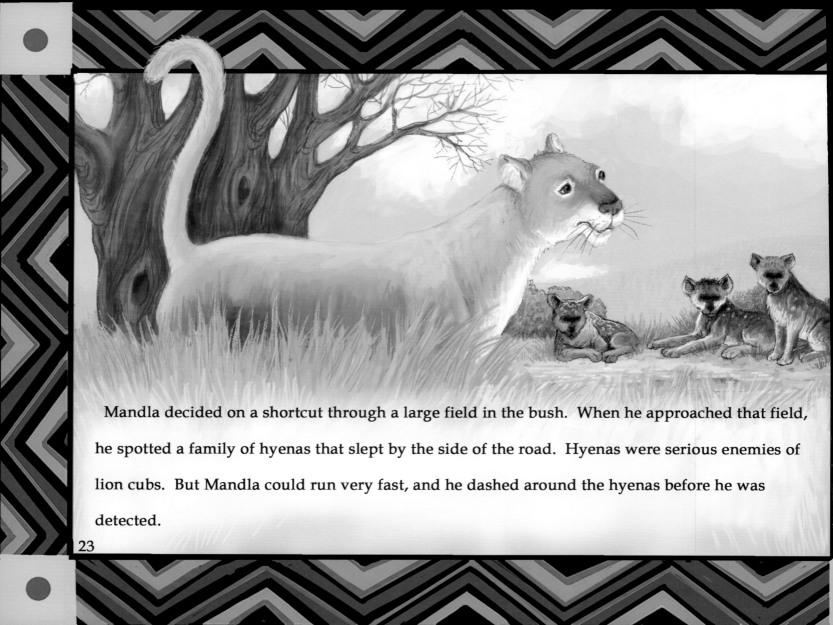

Mandla decided on a shortcut through a large field in the bush. When he approached that field, he spotted a family of hyenas that slept by the side of the road. Hyenas were serious enemies of lion cubs. But Mandla could run very fast, and he dashed around the hyenas before he was detected.

Taki also thought about returning through this field, but he was alarmed by the hyenas and decided on a detour instead.

24

Racing against the sunset, Taki ran on a trail along the Crocodile River. A slow turtle was crossing the trail and, much to the concern of Taki, a crocodile was lurking in the weeds. "Hssssssssss," sounded the crocodile.

25

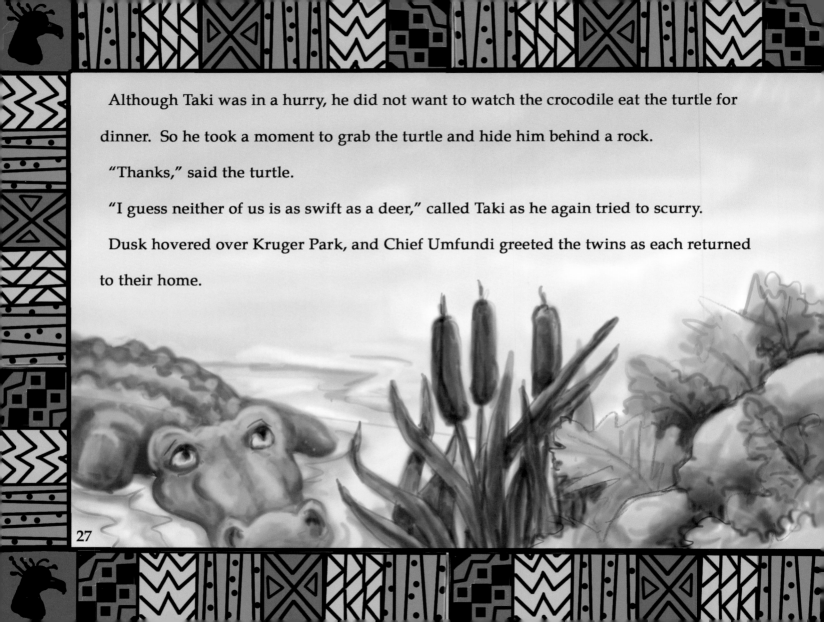

Although Taki was in a hurry, he did not want to watch the crocodile eat the turtle for dinner. So he took a moment to grab the turtle and hide him behind a rock.

"Thanks," said the turtle.

"I guess neither of us is as swift as a deer," called Taki as he again tried to scurry.

Dusk hovered over Kruger Park, and Chief Umfundi greeted the twins as each returned to their home.

27

Vusi paused from his story. He looked to his children.

"Umfundi is going to tell his cubs who will be the next

Chief. Can either of you guess who he has chosen?"

Makalo was always practical, so he shouted,

"Mandla will be Chief.

He is strong, brave and fast."

"I am not so sure," argued Nandi.

Readers and listeners of this story, what do you think?

Who will be Chief?

Vusi continues…

"Sit down, my sons," instructed the Chief. Perched on his shoulder was Lebona, his secretarybird.

31

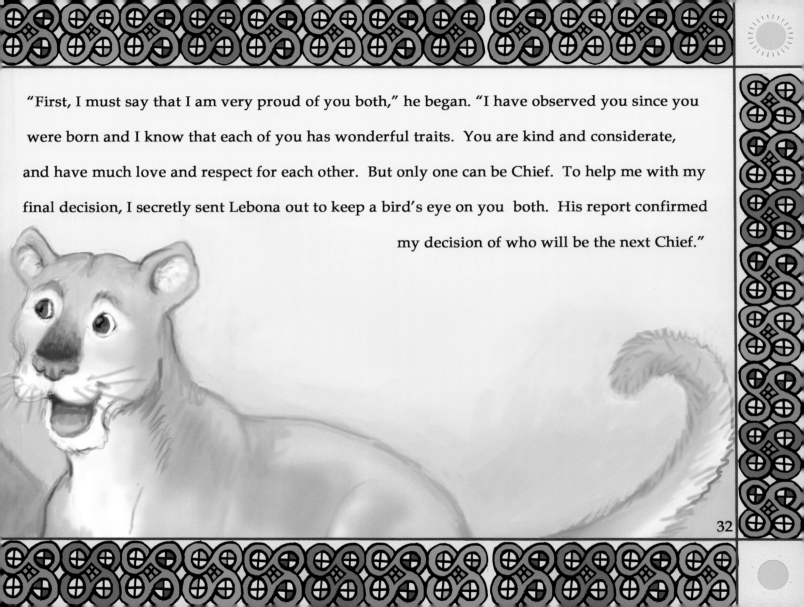

"First, I must say that I am very proud of you both," he began. "I have observed you since you were born and I know that each of you has wonderful traits. You are kind and considerate, and have much love and respect for each other. But only one can be Chief. To help me with my final decision, I secretly sent Lebona out to keep a bird's eye on you both. His report confirmed my decision of who will be the next Chief."

The cubs were fairly relaxed because they assumed they knew the decision.

33

To their surprise, however, Chief Umfundi majestically declared, "The lion to follow me will be Taki."

34

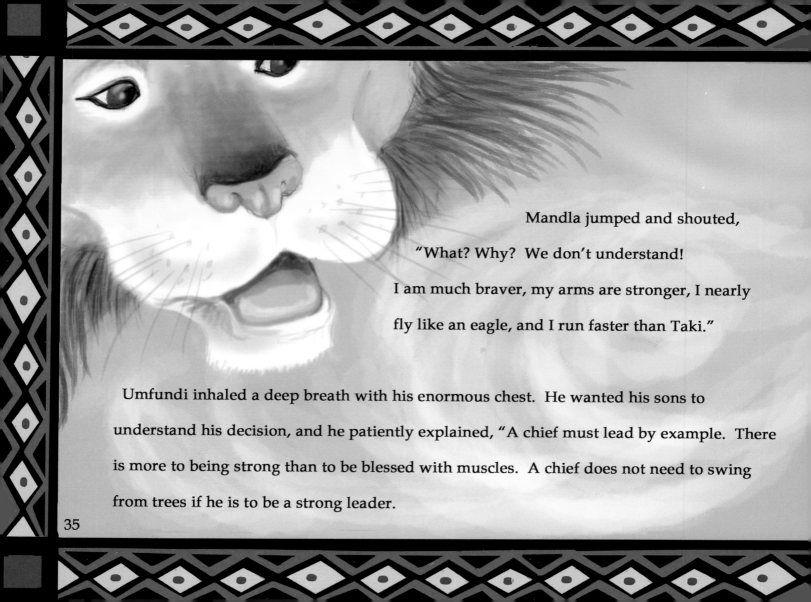

Mandla jumped and shouted,
"What? Why? We don't understand!
I am much braver, my arms are stronger, I nearly
fly like an eagle, and I run faster than Taki."

Umfundi inhaled a deep breath with his enormous chest. He wanted his sons to

understand his decision, and he patiently explained, "A chief must lead by example. There

is more to being strong than to be blessed with muscles. A chief does not need to swing

from trees if he is to be a strong leader.

"A chief must wake up and carry

the weight of his responsibilities

each and every day, and carry

such weight with excitement,

not with burden. In fact,

a good leader hopes that all in his land will

wake up like a lion.

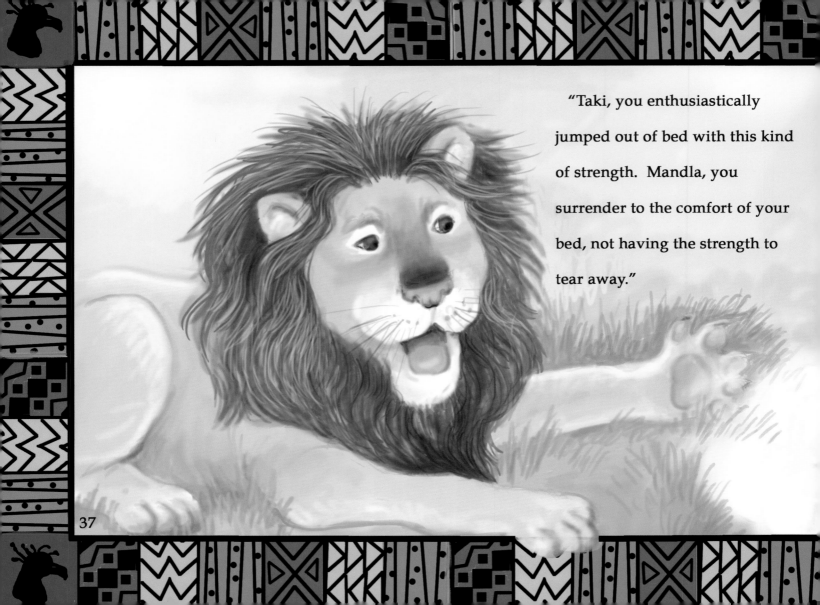

"Taki, you enthusiastically jumped out of bed with this kind of strength. Mandla, you surrender to the comfort of your bed, not having the strength to tear away."

37

38

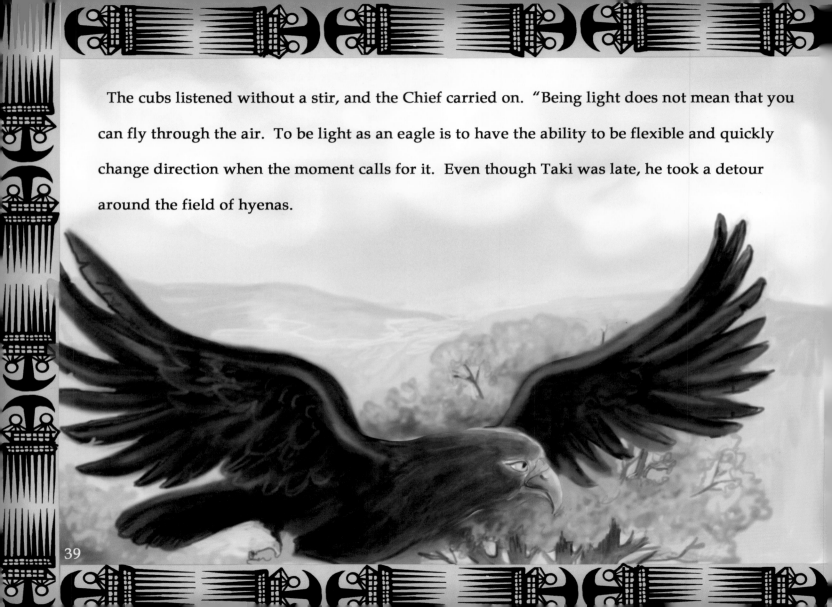

The cubs listened without a stir, and the Chief carried on. "Being light does not mean that you can fly through the air. To be light as an eagle is to have the ability to be flexible and quickly change direction when the moment calls for it. Even though Taki was late, he took a detour around the field of hyenas.

"And to add to that, Taki swiftly ran to assist a turtle in need. Being a fast runner is important when we face a predator, but a great leader need not be the fastest. A great chief must run to help others in need. That is how we are swift as a deer. If our citizens follow this example, then our land will flourish with charity and kindness.

"Finally, let's talk about boldness. I agree that it was brave for Mandla to run past the hyenas. They are very dangerous. But it also takes much courage to stand our ground. Taki, you avoided danger by refusing to swim near the hippopotamus, and that was the right decision. You risked popularity with your friends. Mandla, you told the monkeys that you did not approve of their antics, but you continued to play with them because you did not want to risk exclusion from their group. As Chief, I am sure I have lost favor when my citizens did not like my decisions. But if they are truly the right decisions, the animals will agree in the end."

  Chief Umfundi stood very tall, and for the last time, he repeated, "The next Chief will be Taki. I have spoken."

Vusi lifted his shoulders at his children and said, "*Indaba isiphelile*. Now it

is time for the two of you to perform your chores." Makalo and Nandi jumped to their feet and

darted to their jobs. Vusi could not recall when either of them went to work with such enthusiasm,

conviction and speed. They were certainly as swift as a deer.

Nandi called out, "I need to start dinner." She gathered spices and beans so that she could grind

everything with the hominy corn. Her neighbor friends were playing with their beaded dolls and

they beckoned her to join them. Today, however, Nandi chose to be bold as a leopard and

continue with her cooking.

"I need to tend to the cattle," Makalo called back. "If you need firewood, I can forage for some on my way back." Nandi threw him a puzzled expression, surprised that he offered to perform an extra task.

"I see that look on your face," he responded. "But today I don't feel sluggish. Today, I am as light as an eagle."

In the meantime, Chief Vusi had turned to finish his painting of the lion, the eagle, the leopard and the deer. As his children ran off, he heard them give a little roar.

Vusi glanced back at Nandi and Makalo, and he smiled.

Name translation (in order of appearance):

Makalo = bewilderment

Nandi = sweet

Vusi short for Vusamuzi = father of the household

Taki = be happy

Mandla = strength

Umfundi = spiritual leader

Nomsa = caring one

Lebona = the one who sees

Definitions:
Kraal = a hut village in southern Africa
Kwesukasukela = once upon a time
Springbok biltong = a type of dried, cured meat from a springbok antelope
Indaba isiphelile = the story is finished

COLORING PAGES

People have created art to use on their pottery, clothing, jewelry, blankets, homes, sculptures and on themselves throughout human history. Some designs represent a culture or tribe more than others. In South Africa, the patterns used in the border designs in this book are found throughout the Zulu culture. The colors they choose are usually very bright and vivid. White, black, red, yellow, green, royal blue, brown and orange are the most dominant choices found in their art.

Create your own pattern by choosing one design, called a motif, like a square, triangle, rectangle, circle, zig zag or stripe, and repeat the same motif over and over.

47

48

About Operation Outreach-USA

Operation Outreach-USA (OO-USA) provides free literacy and character education programs to elementary schools across the country.

Because reading is the gateway to success, leveling the learning field for at-risk children is critical. By giving books to children to own, confidence is built and motivated readers are created. OO-USA selects books with messages that teach compassion, respect, and determination. OO-USA involves the school and the home with tools for teachers and parents to nurture and guide children as they learn and grow.

More than one million children in schools in all fifty states have participated in the program thanks to the support of a broad alliance of corporate, foundation, and individual sponsors.

To learn more about Operation Outreach-USA and how to help,
visit www.oousa.org, call 1-800-243-7929, or email info@oousa.org.